AI v. RI

Artificial Intelligence Versus Real Ignorance

Navigating a New Frontier Without Losing Yourself in the Noise

Table of Contents:

The Potential Pitfalls and Ethical Considerations

Chapter 11: The Alpha in the Age of AI - Embracing an Alpha Mentality in a World Dictated by Data

The Difference Between Being an Alpha and a Narcissist in the AI Age

Personal Affirmation: Guarding and Feeding Your Internal Sense of Hope and Ambition in an AI-Driven World

Fire, Suspended *(excerpt)*

Chapter 12: Conclusion and Final Reflections

Summarizing the Key Takeaways: AI Is a Tool that Can Either Propel Us or Inhibit Us Based on How We Use It

Final Thoughts: We Are Seeds in This Newly Tilled Ground of Artificial Intelligence; It's Time to Grow

Personal Farewell: Strap on Your Boots, Harness the Power of Technology, and Let's Do This. Together.

Appendix: Resources for Your AI Journey

Acknowledgments

Introduction

There is a great oak inside us all. Many times our growth is stunted due to the shade that others cast upon us, rather than their help shining or fertilizing what is in us. Your environment will stunt your potential or it can help you grow into a mighty oak. A tree will always gravitate toward the light. However, its growth and potential will always be limited until it gets the proper amount of light and nutrients.

Tim Scholze, Pinnacle Sales Coaching

Hello, dear reader. If you've picked up this book, scrolled to this page, or happened to select it on Audible after some friendly stalking determined it was a fit for you, chances are you're as intrigued, baffled, or even perhaps as skeptical as most are about the tidal wave that is Artificial Intelligence. Welcome to AI v. RI, a deep dive into the exhilarating yet often misunderstood relationship between Artificial Intelligence and human capability.

Purpose of the Book

In today's increasingly automated and data-driven world, Artificial Intelligence (AI) is a term you've likely heard ad nauseam. From the talking points of tech moguls to the worry-filled discussions at the family dinner table, AI evokes a range of emotions—awe, fear, excitement, and skepticism. However, beneath these emotional reactions often lies a wide chasm of Real Ignorance (RI). It's not necessarily a pejorative term; it's an acknowledgment that when it comes to AI, the majority of us don't know what we don't know. And that's what this book aims to rectify.

I write this not as a distant academic, but as someone deeply involved in the application and understanding of AI in the real world. As someone who has been labeled an "alpha," who has climbed the professional ladder, failed, succeeded again, and navigated through the complexities of life and business, I bring a pragmatic lens to this exploration. My journey has been far from straightforward—I've been guided and coached, tried, erred, and learned. From being a $ 50k-a-year salesperson, eventually rising to a high-ranking C-level executive, and from there, moving into entrepreneurship and philanthropy, I've seen the transformative power of intelligent decision-making, often enhanced by intelligent systems.

AI, if harnessed properly, can be a tool for unprecedented advancement. But like any powerful tool, it has its risks, ethics, and governance that we must consider as well. This book will tackle these subjects head-on, sharing not only what I've learned but also what experts in the field have to contribute to our understanding.

What Lies Ahead

This book is structured to take you on a journey, from understanding the basic terms and technologies that underpin AI to exploring its potential impacts on employment, personal development, ethics, and more. We'll dissect myths and confront realities, all with the aim of turning 'Real Ignorance' into 'Real Insight.'

So, if you're ready to navigate this new world where AI intersects with your life, career, and even your sense of self, keep reading. With the right compass as your guide, you can find the true North and have confidence in the future. The future belongs to those willing to learn, adapt, and grow. Those who fail forward, just as the domino must fall to achieve the contagion. Keeping in mind that we are in this together, that together we go far, and individually, we go fast. A domino alone falls. A domino falling forward with others on the quest spurs greater change, pushing lessons onto the next and the next. And in this technological age, understanding AI isn't just a nice-to-have skill—it's a must-have. And, I may just be your huckleberry and your catalyst to breaking the Mustang that is AI.

Okay, my adventuresome spirits. Strap on those boots,, harness the power of technology, and let's do this. Together.

Welcome to AI v. RI.

Chapter 1: The Age of Calculators

In the vast symphony of human progress, every instrument has its moment to shine, and every melody its time to be heard. There was a time when calculators were the misunderstood prodigies in the orchestra of human invention, doubted, debated upon, and even scorned. Yes, scorned. Imagine a time when people genuinely thought calculators would make us intellectually lazy. These handheld devices would replace the need for mental math, for knowing your multiplication tables, for understanding the logic behind long division. We griped about it. We protested. "This will be the death of mental prowess!" cried the critics, pointing fingers at the boxy gadgets with green LED screens.

I get it, you know? Back then, people had to grapple with a new reality. Like staring at a dark sky and wondering if the sun will rise again. Fear overshadowed rationality. And we do that often, don't we? We let fear cloud our judgment and pull us into a loop of negativity and anxiety. When calculators first came onto the scene, we reacted like they were an invading army, a force coming to dismantle our very cognition.

Let's sit with that for a moment. Deeply sit with it. Because this anxiety, this fear, is a powerful thing. It sneaks in like a thief in the night, taking away your peace of mind, your confidence, your vision of a better tomorrow. It whispers, "This is the end of your abilities, the annihilation of your intellect. Get ready for a lifetime of dependency."

How many times have you heard that same voice in your own life? When you felt stuck, maybe in a dead-end job, a failing relationship, or even when confronting your own personal challenges. "You're not going to make it," it hisses, sowing the seed of doubt in the fertile soil of your mind. The fertile soil where hope should be growing.

But let's get something straight. We're not here to nurture that voice of fear. No. We're here to confront it, grab it by the collar, look it straight in the eyes, and tell it, "You're wrong." Because that's exactly what happened with calculators. We looked fear in the eyes and said, "You are wrong."

Contrary to stealing our cognitive abilities, calculators freed us. Yes, they freed us. Freed us to delve into problems and concepts far more complex than we could have imagined. Think about it. We transitioned from worrying about basic arithmetic to solving equations that paved the way for space travel, medical breakthroughs, and technological advances that define the world today. All because calculators took away the grunt work, the tedious calculations, and allowed us to focus on the big picture.

People stopped saying, "It'll do the math for you," and started asking, "What can you do with it?" And the sky was the limit. Physicists began solving problems about the universe, not just the corner grocery store. Engineers started designing bridges that defy the imagination, not just a barn or a house. And kids? Oh, kids started learning calculus in high school, and algebra became a middle school subject.

Have you ever found yourself in a situation where you've been liberated? When the weight on your shoulders was lifted, and you realized your potential was far greater than you ever allowed yourself to imagine? Maybe it was leaving a toxic relationship. Maybe it was quitting a job that consumed you. Maybe it was as simple as deciding to get fit and taking that first step on the treadmill. That's what calculators did for us.

That's when you realize what's possible. That's when the seed buried deep within you doesn't see itself as dead but realizes it's ready to break through the soil, hungry for the sun. For light. For life. For hope.

So, why do we keep making the same mistakes? With every new invention, and every new piece of technology that comes our way, we hear the same old song— "This will make us dumber. This will make us lazier. This will take our jobs away." Just like we did with calculators. But let's learn the lesson, shall we? Let's not be so quick to pass judgment on something that could elevate us to greater heights. Because that's the thing, fear confines you, but hope? Hope is boundless.

We often think we're being cautious, protecting ourselves, protecting our future. But in reality, we're chaining ourselves to a rock that's sinking fast, and we don't even know it. We think it's safer to stay put than to venture into uncharted waters. We cling to the rock as if it will save us. But you know what really happens? We sink. We let opportunities pass by. We let life pass by.

I've seen so many bright minds put a cap on their potential, locking themselves in a cage of their own making, all because of fear. "I can't leave my job; it's stable." "I can't end this relationship; it's comfortable." "I can't try something new; it's risky."

But what if the real risk is not stepping into the unknown? What if the real risk is settling for a life that's less than what you're capable of living? That's the real tragedy, my friend. The unlived life. The untapped potential. And, as my mother once said in a bit of an admonishment toward an intrepid me, feeling stuck in a thankless job while trying to raise two children on my own, no one ever lay on their deathbed and lamented that they had worked harder. Freeing yourself from fear can assist in strengthening the work/life balance because you begin to do it your own way. Pioneer your life, forge your way, author your destiny.

Just like calculators, new technologies offer us the chance to redefine the parameters of our existence. They challenge us to think differently, to step outside our comfort zones, to reach for something greater. And yeah, that's scary. It's scary because we don't know what's on the other side. We can't predict the future. But isn't that the whole point of living? To take risks? To experience the full range of human emotion and capability?

Calculators may be a small part of this tale, a humble instrument in the orchestra, but their story teaches us something vital: that the unknown, the thing we often fear the most, is often the gateway to unimaginable potential.

So, the next time a new piece of technology, an unexpected opportunity, or an uncharted path presents itself, don't look down in fear. Look up with hope. And remember, the best version of you is just waiting for a chance to break free, to break new ground, to solve new problems, and to write new chapters in the book of human progress.

Because you, my friend, are not a finished equation. You're a complex problem that's fascinating to solve, one that changes and evolves, surprising even yourself with the solutions you discover along the way.

Not everyone who holds a calculator can solve a complex mathematical equation, but without one, a capable mind can be severely limited. I know firsthand as I struggled through Personal Finance at Baylor University. I was no mathematician. However, I had a regional genius level IQ and had always been in honors math courses in high school.

Here I was at Baylor, deep in debt with student loans, and I didn't have the money for the Texas Instruments calculator we were required to buy. And so I failed, miserably, trying to make sense of the formulas on my own. Finally, the night before the final exam, I studied with a group of friends, and one with her final at a different time promised to lend me her calculator. They showed me how to navigate this very complex little computer and I tried to apply everything I'd learned up until then to the new knowledge of this device.

Fast forward to a year or two later, as I'm walking the halls of the Hankamer School of Business, the very professor from Personal Finance stops me and says, "Wendi Sanford, you are a legend in my class!" I looked at her in confusion. She went on to explain, "You came into my final exam with a low 50 and you ACED that final. I would have accused you of cheating but you got a higher grade than any other person taking the course." She then told me she has told my story in her classes in order to encourage people to keep trying. She then said, "I have to know, how did you do it?"

To which, I answered, "I couldn't afford the calculator. The night prior to the exam, I was loaned one." I will never forget the expression on her face and how her mouth fell open. I knew she now had an even better story for future classes. She was truly a great teacher, and knowing she used an anecdote from a shared experience with me to encourage others' growth, meant the world to me.

You see, I applied everything she taught me, that I had tried to do without a machine resource and was able to accel because of it. Perhaps those of us who are only now indoctrinated on AI may have a greater capacity to accel at it than those who will rely on its assistance from the very start of their education.

And trust me, in this story, you're the one holding the calculator for the first time after working those equations on your own. You're the one defining the problems worth solving. And that's a powerful place to be.

You may feel like a failure going in. But you may become a legend on your way out.

Chapter 2: A Leap to Artificial Intelligence

If calculators were the opening act in the digital concert that shaped our world, artificial intelligence is undoubtedly the headliner, the star performer that packs the arena and electrifies the air. From the onset, it had us buzzing with both awe and apprehension, turning our gazes to a future we could barely fathom. Would it be utopian or dystopian? Would it spell the zenith of human capability or signify the nadir of our self-inflicted downfall?

It's not surprising that the emergence of AI was greeted with skepticism, as it has been throughout history when any disruptive technology burst onto the scene. Remember how people scoffed at the notion of a horseless carriage? How could an automobile possibly replace the reliable, living, breathing entity that had served us since time immemorial? Then there were the calculators—our good old friends—which were once considered threats to our cognitive faculties.

Brief History of AI and the Skepticism that Surrounded Its Emergence

Artificial intelligence has had its roots dug deep, with pioneers like Alan Turing laying the theoretical groundwork as far back as the 1940s and 50s. Turing postulated that a machine could simulate any human intelligence—a bold statement at the time, one that didn't escape controversy.

The term "artificial intelligence" was coined in 1956 by John McCarthy for the famous Dartmouth Workshop, which is considered the birthing ground of AI as an academic discipline. From then on, AI research took two main paths: one striving for 'applied AI' or expert systems capable of narrow tasks, and the other pursuing 'general AI,' which would possess human-like understanding and consciousness. And with each leap in advancement, whether it was IBM's Deep Blue beating Garry Kasparov at chess or Google's AlphaGo triumphing over human Go champions, society couldn't help but recoil a bit, bracing for an uncertain future. Was the serpent in the digital Eden coiling around us? Afterall, as evidenced by the mark we all walk around branded with, we took a bit out of that apple.

The skeptics found fertile ground in pop culture. Movies like "The Terminator," "The Matrix," and "Ex Machina" depicted a world where AI systems revolt against their creators, usurping control and rendering humanity redundant or even extinct. Every tech billionaire warning about the AI apocalypse was lauded as a soothsayer. Indeed, the fear was palpable, much like the initial resistance to calculators. Would AI systems replace us, and worse, would they become uncontrollable?

Real-World Applications of AI that Have Bettered Our Lives

Yet here we stand, at a time when AI not only augments human capacity but also enriches our lives in numerous ways. Take healthcare, where AI algorithms are used to read and interpret complex medical images, sometimes with greater accuracy than human experts. This doesn't replace doctors; rather, it frees them to perform the deeply human aspects of care that no machine can replicate.

In agriculture, AI-powered drones assess field conditions, predict crop yields, and even assist with planting and harvesting. This not only makes food production more efficient but also paves the way for sustainable practices that will benefit future generations.

How about the very fabric of human connection? Language translation services powered by AI are demolishing linguistic barriers, enabling cross-cultural exchanges that enrich our global tapestry. For the differently-abled, AI-driven tools are life-changing, from real-time sign language interpretation to mobility solutions.

Personal Reflection: Breaking Free from the Fears Surrounding AI, for a More Productive Future

So why do we hold onto our fears like a protective talisman? Perhaps it's a survival instinct—an evolutionary mechanism to shield us from perceived threats. But the irony is that this very fear can inhibit our survival and growth, trapping us in a paradox of our own making.

It's time we broke free, just like we did with calculators. The calculator did not herald the end of human intelligence; it was an augmentation, a tool that extended our cognitive reach. AI is poised to be another such tool, albeit more potent and versatile. But just like a calculator, it's what we do with it that defines its value.

If we continue to regard AI as a rival or a looming existential threat, we risk diminishing its potential as a beneficial extension of human capability. It's when we partner with AI, rather than pit ourselves against it, that we can truly unlock its promises.

Skepticism has its place; it can be a healthy reaction that prevents heedless advancement. But let's ensure our skepticism doesn't paralyze us or mire us in dystopian fantasies. It's crucial to regulate AI, to instate ethical guidelines, and to be aware of potential pitfalls, but it's equally crucial to embrace its vast potential.

In breaking free from these fears, we are also setting ourselves free—to explore, to innovate, and to usher in an era where human-machine symbiosis could solve some of the most pressing challenges of our time.

If calculators were about lifting the burden of basic computation to open the gateway to higher forms of mathematics and engineering, then AI is about transcending our cognitive and physical limitations to glimpse possibilities beyond our imagination. Whether it's combating climate change, solving complex medical mysteries, or exploring distant galaxies, AI stands as a beacon of potential—only if we dare to venture toward it.

As we stand at this threshold, let's not recoil in fear but stride forth with cautious optimism. Our narrative with AI is not pre-written; it is a dynamic script that we're authoring each day, with every choice and every interaction. And as long as we, the human component, act as responsible stewards, as ethical operators, then this story is one of limitless possibility.

Our history with calculators teaches us that technology is not a zero-sum game, where gains in computational power equate to losses in human relevance. In fact, it's quite the opposite. Each technological advance offers us a new lens through which to view our world, ourselves, and our future.

So, let's hold that lens up to the light and peer through, for what we'll find on the other side is not a foreboding shadow but a spectrum of colors—vibrant, diverse, and waiting to be explored.
AI is not a Pandora's Box of unforeseen calamities; it's a treasure chest, teeming with potential jewels that could adorn the tapestry of human civilization. But to find these jewels, we have to open the chest. We have to take the leap.

And you know what? I think we're ready.

Chapter 3: AI vs. Real Ignorance

Let's now touch upon the elephant in the room, given the title of this book and the aggressive nature with which it can be interpreted. We've got something to dissect here that has been bothering me and probably you too—Ignorance. Oh, that term. That word that, for some reason, has managed to still exist, to still plague us, in an age where information is literally at our fingertips. Do you have a phone? Do you have Wi-Fi? Then, you've got the world's wisdom at your disposal. But what do we do? We still stick our heads in the sand and pretend the world is flat. Pythagoras be damned. That's not just ignorance, that's an affront to human intelligence.

The Concept of Ignorance in the Age of Information

So, here we are, in this swirling vortex of human advancement. We've got these tremendous tools, this amazing technology—hell, you can ask a question aloud in your room, and a piece of plastic and circuits will answer you back. It's like living in a Sci-Fi novel, except it's real. But still, here we are, with people believing the Earth is flat, that vaccines are a government conspiracy, and that the moon landing was faked. I mean, come on, people. If ignorance was an Olympic sport, we'd have a lot of gold medalists by now.

Yeah, I get it. You're thinking, "But isn't this the information age? Isn't that supposed to make us smarter?" Ah, see, that's the double-edged sword. Information is everywhere, but so is misinformation. The internet is both a library and a dumpster, and too many folks can't tell the difference between the two. But here's where it gets real—Artificial Intelligence. Yes, the same AI we were talking about before. Let's explore that.

How AI Can Help Us Eradicate Ignorance and Become More Informed Individuals

Before you roll your eyes and think I'm going full techno-optimist on you (assuming you haven't yet), hear me out. Imagine a tool, driven by AI, that helps you filter through the trash and gets you what you need, what's real. Algorithms that are designed to recognize credible sources, that sort out peer-reviewed studies from opinion blogs disguised as journalism.

Think about how much smarter we'd be if we weren't wasting our brain cells on nonsense. How much more wealth we would accrue if we weren't wasting money here and there on get-rich-quick schemes and promotions touting AI prowess? It's already happening. AI systems are getting better at fact-checking, summarizing complex documents, and even detecting fake news. It's not about the machine telling us what to think; it's about the machine helping us think better.

Here's a life lesson for you: Don't fight what empowers you. We fear AI is going to take over, going to make us obsolete. But why? Why not see it as another tool, a partner, in our journey towards betterment? It's all about perspective. EVERYTHING is about perspective.

Life Lesson: Let's Stop Assigning Blame to Technology and Begin Understanding Its Transformative Potential

Listen up. This is big. Just like we have to stop depending upon other people for our hope and our validation, we also have to stop blaming technology for our shortcomings. You think calculators made us dumb? No, they freed us to tackle even bigger mathematical problems. Computers didn't make us less social; they gave us the tools to connect globally. So, why would AI make us obsolete?

If you're burying your talents and ignoring your growth potential, don't blame the machine. The machine isn't going to replace you. You'll be replaced by the guy who knows how to use that machine to be a hundred times more efficient, more creative, and yes, even more human. So dig deep. Don't let ignorance define your world. Learn, adapt, and for heaven's sake, use the technology that can make you better.

Remember this. AI isn't your enemy. Ignorance is. Ignorance that refuses to adapt, that refuses to grow, that drags us all down into a pit where innovation dies and aspirations wither. You got this incredible brain; it's time to use it. Couple it with the artificial brain that's all around you, and then go be freaking spectacular.

So, straighten up. Look that challenge in the eye. Do you see ignorance surrounding you with whispers of doubt? Don't give those voices a platform and a mic. Give it all a nod and say, "Not today, you don't stand a chance." Harness the AI that you've got at your disposal. Be the informed, empowered individual you were always destined to be. Your path is forming in front of you, waiting for your direction but surrounding you with a more intriguing terrain than you could ever imagine.

And plenty of people will tell you that you can't. That's fine. And unavoidable. That is real ignorance in its very form. Just never, ever let anyone cause you to believe you can't. Of course, you can. You have it all within you, and it's not a piece of you that can be taken, broken, or restricted. Ignorance is a choice. Choose intelligence, choose growth. Choose to be spectacularly, undeniably, irrevocably informed. The ignorant actively choose the opposite, with an invigorating determination to make themselves elite on the conviction of some moral compass. Choose to fly, be a maverick, a fighter pilot…and let AI be your wingman in this incredible flight.

And AI can be my wingman anytime.

Chapter 4: The AI Ecosystem

Alright, my friend, brace yourself. We're diving into the nitty-gritty, the details, the under-the-hood stuff that fuels this wild ride we're on with Artificial Intelligence. You know, AI isn't just one thing; it's a whole ecosystem. It's like saying "animals" when you've got everything from a goldfish to an elephant. They're all animals, but buddy, you wouldn't use a goldfish to plow a field, would you?

Different Types of AI: Machine Learning, Neural Networks, NLP

First up, let's talk about the types of AI that are powering this revolution. If you're going to navigate this world, you better know your way around it.

Machine Learning

So, you remember when you were a kid, right? You touch a hot stove, and you learn not to do it again. That's learning. Now, machine learning is the same concept but for computers. You feed the algorithm a bunch of data and let it figure out the patterns. It's like training a dog, but instead of "sit" and "stay," you're teaching it to predict stock market trends or recommend a movie you'd like.

Machine learning is broad, but the crux of it lies in its ability to adapt and improve over time. It doesn't just follow a fixed set of rules. Instead, it evolves. You don't need to babysit it all the time, rewriting lines of code. You give it the right environment to learn, and it goes off to the races. It's what powers a lot of those personalized recommendations you see when you're shopping online, what makes search engines smarter, and what helps medical researchers analyze massive sets of data for patterns humans might miss.

Neural Networks

Next up, we've got neural networks. If machine learning is the animal kingdom, neural networks are like the human brain of the operation—complex, nuanced, and incredibly capable. These are algorithms designed to recognize patterns. They interpret sensory data through a kind of machine perception, labeling, and clustering of raw input. If machine learning is a toddler figuring out shapes, neural networks are a detective piecing together a complex puzzle.

These networks form the backbone of what's commonly referred to as "deep learning," which is responsible for some of the most exciting breakthroughs in AI. This is where things like image and speech recognition, machine translation, and even autonomous vehicles come into play.

Natural Language Processing (NLP)

Now, let's talk about one of my favorite branches of AI—Natural Language Processing, or NLP for short. Ever used a voice-activated assistant? Ever chatted with a customer service bot online? Yep, that's NLP working its magic. It's the field of AI that focuses on the interaction between computers and us, puny humans, through natural language.

The ultimate objective of NLP is to read, decipher, understand, and make sense of human language in a way that is valuable. That's no small feat, considering language is full of nuance, context, idioms, and the etymological backing I have obsessed over as a lifelong hobby. This is what allows machines to understand us, to chat with us, and eventually, even to write whole chapters like the one you're reading now. NLP is the bridge between machines understanding numbers and understanding words, and let's face it, we need that bridge to communicate.

Now that we've covered these basics, we're going to dig into some real-world stuff in the upcoming sections. I'm talking about the impacts of these AI types on healthcare, transportation, finance, and more. I'll even give you a personal rundown of how I navigate this complex landscape, one AI-powered decision at a time.

Stick around, because this is just the beginning. I told you, we're going deep, so grab your diving gear. The ocean of AI is vast, my friend, but I promise you, it's worth exploring.

Applications and Impacts on Various Sectors: Healthcare, Transportation, Finance

Whew, alright! Now that we've got our bearings on the different creatures in the AI zoo, let's take a safari through the jungles of real-world applications. Because let's be honest, all the techy stuff is neat, but what we really care about is how it changes our lives. Strap in, because we're diving into three sectors that touch practically everyone's life: healthcare, transportation, and finance.

Healthcare: A Doctor in Your Pocket

First up, let's talk healthcare. Anyone who's ever had a sick loved one—or heck, has been sick themselves—knows how important quality care is. Well, AI is here, and it's got its stethoscope ready.

Imagine walking into a doctor's office where advanced machine learning algorithms have already analyzed your medical history, lab results, and even genomic data. By the time you sit down with the doctor, they're not just informed; they're ready to discuss a highly personalized treatment plan.

And let's talk diagnostics. AI-powered tools like IBM's Watson can analyze the meaning and context of structured and unstructured data in clinical notes and reports. Machine learning algorithms can spot abnormalities in X-rays or MRI scans sometimes even better than the human eye. It's like having Sherlock Holmes inspect your medical reports, leaving no clue unnoticed, and no kidney stone unturned.

And for those in rural or remote areas? Telemedicine backed by AI can provide life-saving diagnoses when a specialist is miles away. The revolution here isn't just in the treatment; it's in the accessibility and equality of care. AI breaks down barriers, literally saving lives that might otherwise be lost.

Transportation: Where We're Going, We Don't Need Roads

Alright, jump out of the doc's chair and hop into a car—except in this car, you're not driving. Yep, I'm talking about autonomous vehicles. Now, I know what you're thinking: "No way I'm letting a robot drive me around!" Hold your horses, cowboy. These aren't just any robots; these are robots trained on millions, if not billions, of miles of road, driving conditions, and those unpredictable elements we call "other drivers."

Neural networks power these autonomous machines, teaching them how to navigate complex road networks, interpret traffic signs, and even understand the subtleties of human behavior, like when a pedestrian is likely to cross the street. Sure, they're not perfect, and there's a whole ethical can of worms to sort through, but the potential here? It's transformative. Reduced traffic, fewer accidents, better fuel efficiency. And for the visually impaired, the elderly, or anyone who can't drive? Freedom, plain and simple.

Finance: Your Money's Best Friend

Last but not least, let's talk about where AI is helping us with something we all love and stress about: money. As aforementioned, I struggle with personal finance coursework and I continue to struggle with the discipline behind it while navigating life with two children and a single income, albeit, a good one. In the financial sector, machine learning is like a superhero with an Excel spreadsheet. Algorithmic trading? That's old news. Now we've got robo-advisors who can manage and optimize your investment portfolio in real-time. These aren't mindless number-crunchers; these are sophisticated algorithms analyzing market trends, global events, and economic indicators, all to make smarter investment choices.

And let's not forget fraud detection. Gone are the days when a scammer could make a couple of dodgy transactions and vanish into the ether. Modern AI algorithms can spot the slightest irregularities in spending patterns, flagging potential fraud faster than you can say "identity theft." And they learn from each event, making them increasingly efficient at spotting risks.

But what about the little guy, the everyday person just trying to budget and save? AI has your back too. Budgeting apps now leverage machine learning to analyze your spending habits, providing personalized advice on saving money. It's like having a financial advisor in your pocket but without the awkward chit-chat and business attire.

And there you have it! Three fields getting turned on their heads, thanks to AI. We're talking about changes that affect your health, how you get from point A to B, and what happens to your hard-earned income. And that, my friend, is just the tip of the iceberg. Up next, I'll give you a personal rundown on how I navigate this convoluted, intricate, yet profoundly promising world of

AI. One choice, one risk, one opportunity at a time. Stay tuned.

Personal Account: Navigating the Complex World of AI, One Choice at a Time

Alright, let's get real for a moment. Enough of the generalities; let's talk specifics. I want to take you back to a time in my own life when AI could have rewritten my story, changing the trajectory of my career in a way that I could only have dreamed of.

Picture it: A mother with two young children, tired of working for others in marketing and hearing the question asked time and again, did I have the bandwidth to help their company the way I was helping my employer? I had a great job title as the Director of Marketing for an ER, but I was making $30k. I decided to start a small business. A local marketing agency that could do it better than the canned national companies. I could add the personal touch, the collaborations with other local businesses and so much more. I had the skills, the passion, and the hustle. What I didn't have was a knack for business analytics, marketing trends, or risk management. Long story short? The business didn't make it past its second birthday. The passion was there, but the lack of insights into business scalability and consumer behavior nailed the coffin shut.

Now let's rewind the tape but add a dash of AI into the mix.

My First Agency

The Difference AI Could Have Made

Had AI been around and accessible, predictive algorithms could have analyzed market trends and consumer behaviors, guiding me toward a profitable niche. Machine learning tools could have sifted through piles of data to recommend optimal pricing strategies. Sentiment analysis could have gauged customer reactions to different branding strategies, helping me fine-tune my message and eliminate some of the setbacks to scalability. And let's not forget automated financial management to keep the business on a sustainable path.

Automated tools could have managed my social media platforms, using machine learning to post content at the times it's most likely to be seen and engaged with. And oh, how I could have used AI-driven design software to quickly generate and iterate designs based on client feedback and preferences. A business that was doomed for lack of data could have not just survived but thrived.

A Catalyst, Not a Crutch

I want you to understand something important: AI isn't a crutch for human inadequacy. It's a catalyst for human potential. It's not about what we can't do; it's about what we can do when empowered by intelligent tools. Had I had AI at my disposal, my career trajectory could have soared. I would have been making choices not based on gut feeling or intuition—which, don't get me wrong, have their place—but on hard, actionable data.

The World We Live in Now

Fast-forward to today. AI is here, and it's glorious. I'm back in the game, running a new venture. Only this time, I'm armed to the teeth with AI-driven tools. From data analytics to automated customer service to intelligent content generation—AI is my wingman. And let me tell you, business is booming.

So here's the moral of the story, folks: Don't just dip your toes in the AI waters. Dive in. The tools are there; they're accessible and more user-friendly than ever. No, they won't run your business for you, but they'll give you the insights and the power to run it like never before. This is our reality, a world teeming with untapped potential, ready to be unlocked by AI.

And as for fear? Let's convert it into fuel. Fear is the mind-killer, sure. But it's also a sign that you're standing at the edge of your comfort zone. Take the leap, and let AI be your parachute.

So, my friends, how will you navigate this complex but enthralling labyrinth of opportunities that AI brings? Remember, we're not talking about some future utopia; we're talking about the here and now. Your choices matter. One intelligent decision at a time, you too can redefine your own story.

And that's a wrap for Chapter 4! Up next, we'll explore the ethical dimensions of AI—a Pandora's box that's as intriguing as it is important. Stay with me; the journey is just getting started.

Chapter 5: Automation Anxiety

The Fear of AI Replacing Human Jobs

Ah, automation anxiety. The fear that kept our ancestors awake at night as they eyed the steam engine and the cotton gin with suspicion, and the same fear that has many of us casting wary glances at AI today. You might be wondering how this relates to Chapter 1 where we talked about the advent of calculators. Well, stick around, because we're about to come full circle.

Remember the resistance the calculator met when it was first introduced? Some mathematicians thought it was the end of "real" arithmetic. They feared that people would become dumb automatons, blindly punching in numbers and losing all ability to calculate. Of course, that's not what happened. What did happen is that we gained a tool that helped us manage complex calculations more efficiently, allowing us to focus on higher-order problem-solving.

The same applies to AI. The panic, though understandable, is largely misplaced. However, let's clarify one thing: Yes, AI is automating tasks and, in some instances, entire job roles. This is true, and to deny it would be an exercise in naivety. But what people often forget is that the roles being replaced are largely mechanical and repetitive. They are roles that can, and arguably should, be automated so that we can aim our human faculties at more complex, creative pursuits.

The Real Threat: Choosing Ignorance Over Intelligence

Now, let's get to the heart of the matter. Your job is far more likely to be replaced by someone who chooses to wield AI as a tool for increasing productivity, not by AI itself. The real threat here isn't artificial intelligence; it's real ignorance. Ignorance is the refusal to adapt, to grow, to step out of your comfort zone and to embrace the future. Ironically, those who lose their jobs due to automation are more likely to remain stuck in this state of ignorance, stagnating rather than evolving.

The individuals who get left behind will often find a convenient scapegoat in AI. "It took our jobs," they'll say, mimicking the doomsday language that has been around for centuries whenever a new technology hits the scene. In blaming AI, they absolve themselves of the responsibility to adapt, to learn, and to grow. It's easier to be the victim than to become the victor.

Ignorance is Bliss, Or Is It?

As the saying goes, perhaps ignorance is bliss. Maybe these individuals, stuck in their ways, will be blissfully unaware of the choices they could have made, the pathways they could have explored. Maybe they'll sleep better at night thinking that their plight was unavoidable, that they're the casualties of technological progress rather than of their own unwillingness to adapt.

But here's the twist: Just because you're blissfully unaware doesn't mean you're actually blissful. Ignorance is a short-term anesthesia that wears off when you're confronted by the harsh realities of life— unemployment, unfulfilled potential, the gnawing feeling that you could be doing so much more. Blaming AI for your woes might offer a momentary sense of relief, but it won't solve the problem. Only choosing intelligence—both real and artificial—can do that.

And remember, intelligence is not a zero-sum game. In making room for artificial intelligence, we're not negating the need for human intelligence. Rather, we're augmenting it, elevating it to new levels of capability and potential. And therein lies the choice: Do we wallow in ignorance, or do we strive for an intelligent coexistence with technology?

So, while the fear of AI "taking our jobs" is a real and pressing concern for many, perhaps the focus should be less on what we stand to lose and more on what we stand to gain. In the next section of this chapter, we will explore why embracing AI could actually be the key to job security in the modern world.

Statistical Insights: AI as a Job Enhancer Rather Than a Job Killer

Ah, statistics, the language of reality. Or at least, as close to reality as we can objectively get. Numbers have a charming way of cutting through the noise and getting straight to the point. And when it comes to AI and jobs, the numbers tell a fascinating story—one that even the staunchest skeptics might find hard to ignore.

The Numbers Don't Lie

According to various studies, it's estimated that AI could add as much as $15.7 trillion to the global economy by 2030. That's not a figure to scoff at. But let's break it down a bit further. What does that economic growth mean for jobs? Well, the World Economic Forum suggests that while 75 million jobs might be displaced by AI and automation by 2022, another 133 million new roles could emerge. Simple arithmetic tells us that results in a net positive of 58 million jobs.

Yes, you read that right: a net positive. For every job that's eliminated, nearly two could be created. Those are odds even a Vegas bookie would envy.

Job Enhancement: A Case Study

Let's look at healthcare, for example. Contrary to the doomsday prophecies, AI has not replaced doctors or nurses. Instead, it's given them superpowers. AI can process and analyze medical data in seconds, something that would take a human hours, if not days, to accomplish. This frees up medical professionals to do what they do best—care for patients. Surgical robots guided by human hands are more precise, diagnostic algorithms detect diseases earlier, and administrative tasks are streamlined, allowing for more human-to-human interaction.

Doctors are not being replaced; they're being enhanced. Their jobs are becoming less about rote memorization and mechanical skills and more about problem-solving, emotional intelligence, and ethical decision-making—skills that are deeply, profoundly human.

What This Means for the Skeptic

If you're a skeptic reading this, consider that embracing AI doesn't mean you're relinquishing your humanity; you're elevating it. AI can take care of the mundane tasks, leaving you with the freedom to innovate, to create, and to make the ethical and emotional decisions that machines are far from capable of making. But to unlock these benefits, you need to be willing to take the first step: you need to be willing to give AI a chance.

You see, even for the skeptic, AI has a bright side, a silver lining in the cloud of automation anxiety. It's not about man vs. machine; it's about man and machine. Together, working in harmony, we can accomplish feats that are not just additive but multiplicative. One plus one can equal three, but only if we choose intelligence over ignorance, only if we see AI as an ally rather than an adversary.

So, to the skeptic, I say: Give it a chance. Let go of the fear and embrace the future. Because, in this ever-changing landscape, adaptability isn't just a useful skill; it's a survival skill. In the final section of this chapter, we'll delve deeper into how we can practically navigate this era of rapid technological advancements without losing our essence.

Personal Motivation: Equip Yourself with the Skills to Coexist with AI, Rather Than Compete Against It

As we stand at this crossroads of history, gazing into the kaleidoscope of possibilities that the future holds, it's understandable to feel a little uneasy. Let me share a moment from my own life—a pivotal experience that starkly revealed the necessity of adapting to the age of AI.

Years ago, I found myself stuck in a job that seemed increasingly irrelevant. Every day, it became clearer that the tasks I was performing could easily be automated. I remember sitting at my desk, meticulously generating reports that no one seemed to read, typing out emails that could easily be replaced by an automated system. I felt obsolete, and it scared me. It was my own moment of 'automation anxiety.'

The fear was paralyzing, but it was also enlightening. I could choose to stay in a state of 'real ignorance,' dismissing AI as the villain of my life story. Or, I could arm myself with the very skills that would make me indispensable in an AI-driven world. I chose the latter. I spent nights and weekends learning about data analytics, familiarizing myself with machine learning, and even dabbling in coding. But most importantly, I started valuing the skills that AI couldn't replicate— empathy, creativity, ethical decision-making. Slowly but surely, I transformed myself from a replaceable cog in a machine to a key player driving that machine.

Fast forward to today, and I find myself in a career that's not just surviving the age of AI, but thriving in it. And it was all possible because I chose to adapt, to learn, to coexist with AI.

Your Path Forward

So, what's the takeaway? The machines are coming, whether we like it or not. But they're not coming for us; they're coming for our mundane tasks, our inefficiencies, our errors. That leaves us with two choices: We can let automation anxiety paralyze us, content to live in blissful ignorance while the world passes us by. Or we can seize this unprecedented opportunity to elevate ourselves, to become more creative, more empathetic, and more human than ever before.

Equip yourself with the kind of intelligence that's genuinely irreplaceable. Learn to work with AI, understand its language, and most importantly, excel in the areas where it falls short. Forge a symbiotic relationship with technology, and you won't just survive the coming wave—you'll ride it.

As we close this chapter, remember this: Your job is only as secure as your willingness to adapt, learn, and grow. In a world increasingly influenced by artificial intelligence, choosing real intelligence is your best bet for a fulfilling, secure career.

So, let's move forward, not in fear but in anticipation, not in competition with AI but in collaboration with it. After all, the future belongs to those who are willing to share it.
Onward, to a world where man and machine coexist, each amplifying the other's strengths, each covering the other's weaknesses. In the next chapter, we'll explore more deeply how this harmonious relationship can shape societies and perhaps even redefine what it means to be human.

Chapter 6: The Harmonic Convergence—Man and Machine

In the early years of AI development, futurists, and science fiction writers painted pictures of dystopian worlds where machines ran rampant, enslaving their human creators or worse, annihilating them. These narratives have lingered in our collective psyche, but as we look around us today, the reality is more nuanced and far more positive. In this chapter, we delve into how AI and humans can coalesce into a harmonic convergence—each entity amplifying the other's capabilities to create a society that is more equitable, efficient, and perhaps even enlightened.

The Creative Engine

Consider the field of design, which has often been touted as the playground of the human imagination—a space where AI could never truly replicate the bounds of human creativity. While it's true that the nuances of human ingenuity can't easily be coded into an algorithm, AI can become a tool that removes the mundane tasks from the designer's workflow. Imagine software that can rapidly prototype hundreds of logo designs based on certain parameters, leaving the designer free to focus on fine-tuning the one that sparks creative joy. This is not a distant future but a present reality.

Ethical Compass in a Digital World

AI's capabilities are not limited to data crunching and automation. There is a growing field of research around "ethical AI." While machines can't possess morals, they can be programmed to follow ethical guidelines, making our systems more just and equitable. For example, an AI algorithm in criminal justice could be designed to flag potential bias in sentencing, offering a safeguard against human prejudices.

Personalized Medicine for All

Even in the field of healthcare, a sector most personal and human, AI has a role to play. AI algorithms are revolutionizing diagnostics, treatment planning, and even patient care. Imagine a world where your medical treatment is tailored not just to your symptoms but your genetic makeup, lifestyle, and even your mental state. AI can parse through millions of data points to provide medical recommendations that are incredibly personalized, taking the healthcare experience to a new dimension of effectiveness.

The Learning Revolution

Education is another sector where the fusion of AI and human effort is leading to some inspiring breakthroughs. Adaptive learning platforms can modify the teaching material in real-time based on the student's performance, ensuring that each learner moves at their own optimized pace. Teachers can then spend more time on one-on-one interactions, addressing the emotional and psychological needs of their students.

The Democratization of Expertise

One of the most profound impacts of this harmonic convergence is the democratization of expertise. With the help of AI, specialized knowledge in fields like law, medicine, or engineering is becoming accessible to the average person. Online platforms powered by sophisticated algorithms can provide preliminary legal advice, medical diagnoses, or even architectural plans, leveling the playing field and empowering individuals to make informed decisions.

Preparing for Harmonic Coexistence

The road to this harmonic convergence is not without its bumps. It requires vigilance in how we design and implement AI systems. But it also necessitates a change in mindset. Instead of viewing AI as a competitor, we must look at it as a collaborator—a digital counterpart that handles computational tasks with machine efficiency, leaving us free to excel at uniquely human tasks such as emotional intelligence, ethical reasoning, and creative expression.

This isn't just about optimizing industries; it's about optimizing human potential. As we go forward into this uncertain yet exciting future, we have the opportunity to redefine what it means to work, to learn, and to live.

By fostering this harmonic relationship with AI, we have the potential to usher in an era of unprecedented global progress—solving complex problems, elevating human creativity, and achieving a level of societal well-being that was previously unimaginable.
So here's to the promise of a future where man and machine coexist not as adversaries but as partners, each bringing their unique set of skills to the table, each filling gaps the other cannot. In such a world, the possibilities are not just additive; they are exponential.

And as we move into this future, let us not be mired in fear or skepticism but propelled by curiosity and a shared sense of purpose. For in this harmonic convergence of man and machine, we may just find the best version of ourse

Chapter 7: Navigating the AI Jungle

From Pied Pipers to Paradigms

As AI continues to pervade every facet of our lives, the burgeoning interest in understanding, implementing, and profiting from this technology is understandable. Our social media feeds, email inboxes, and even physical mailboxes are flooded with promises of "Master AI in 30 Days!" or "Become an AI Engineer Now!" But how do we sift through the noise to find the melody? How do we separate the wheat from the chaff, the genuine from the superficial, the pedagogues from the Pied Pipers?

A Sea of Options—Making Sense of It

There's no dearth of AI courses, workshops, and tutorials available, both online and offline. They range from university-accredited courses to fly-by-night YouTube channels. While the democratization of education is a boon, it also opens the floodgates for misinformation, pseudo-expertise, and outright scams.

So how do you navigate this maze? The first step is self-awareness. Know what you want to achieve with AI. Is it a career change you're eyeing, or are you an entrepreneur looking to integrate AI into your business? Or perhaps, you're just intellectually curious. Your goals will help define your educational path.

The Self-Taught Journey

For those willing to embark on the self-taught journey, the internet is a treasure trove of resources. Websites like Coursera, Udacity, and edX offer courses from top-tier universities on AI and machine learning. Forums like Reddit and Stack Overflow allow you to engage with others who are also navigating the AI ecosystem. GitHub repositories provide real-world code examples, and arXiv and Google Scholar offer free access to research papers. In this age of information, your greatest teacher could be your own initiative.

But as you do this, remember to always check the credentials of your sources. Just as you wouldn't take financial advice from someone mired in debt, don't take AI education from someone whose expertise is suspect. Check for academic qualifications, industry experience, or, at the very least, a body of work that supports their claims.

Following the Right Leaders

Before following any self-proclaimed AI "guru," research their past work, read reviews, or even better, talk to people who have taken their courses or read their material. This isn't foolproof, but it significantly lowers your risk of being led astray.

The Resilience of Failure

Let's face it; not all that glitters is gold. You may sign up for a course that promises the world and delivers an atlas—a shrunken, distorted version of what should be a vast landscape of knowledge. You might invest time and money in learning an AI programming language only to find out that the industry has shifted its preference to another. Here's where the resilience of failure comes in. In the world of AI and tech, failure is not a full stop; it's a comma.

What matters is not that you failed but that you learned something in the process. Maybe you learned to vet your sources better or gained insights into what area of

AI genuinely interests you. Perhaps you discovered that you have an aptitude for data analysis, a crucial skill in AI, even if you didn't become proficient in neural networks. In the grand scheme, these are not failures; they are signposts on your journey.

The Wisdom of Iterative Learning

In this fast-evolving field, the most successful individuals are not those who never fail but those who keep iterating their learning process—each time with more wisdom, focus, and understanding. Each stumble is a step forward, each failure a disguised lesson, each restart a new path to potential mastery.

Endnote

It's easy to get swept up in the wave of AI enthusiasm and equally easy to get disillusioned when things don't go as planned. What we need to remember is that the journey into AI is not a sprint; it's a marathon. It's an ongoing process of learning, adapting, and growing. Be cautious, but not cynical. Be enthusiastic, but not gullible. Follow, but don't be led blindly. And above all, when you fall, rise again—with more wisdom and a refined roadmap.

Navigating the AI ecosystem requires a balance of enthusiasm and skepticism, a keen eye for authenticity, and above all, the resilience to learn from both successes and setbacks. This balanced approach won't just serve you well in mastering AI; it will be an invaluable life skill in this increasingly complex world. And as you learn, iterate, and perhaps even master AI, you don't just add a skill to your resume; you add a layer of nuanced understanding to your worldview, making you not just a student of AI, but a scholar of modern life.

Resources for Learning the New Literacy of AI

In a world that's constantly evolving, especially within the realms of technology and artificial intelligence, the capacity to learn is one of the most valuable assets one can have. It's often said that we're all students in the classroom of life. But with the breakneck speed at which AI is advancing, the question becomes: Where do we even start? Although the field is nascent, and it's rare to find individuals who can claim decades of expertise in AI, that doesn't mean there aren't reliable resources to guide us on our journey to literacy in this new domain.

Setting the Right Mindset

Before diving into specifics, let's set the stage for your educational journey. AI is still a young field; it's burgeoning, changing, and expanding in ways we can't entirely predict. That means your education in AI will be less about mastering a fixed body of knowledge and more about developing a flexible skill set that allows you to adapt and grow with the field. Keeping an "astute eye, discipline, and a collaborative willingness to share wins and losses," as you aptly put it, will serve you well on this journey.

Online Courses

There's no shortage of online courses to choose from. Platforms like Coursera, Udacity, and edX offer specialized AI and machine learning courses that are accredited by universities like Stanford, MIT, and IBM. These platforms offer the chance to learn from real experts in the field and to gain a certification that can help you professionally.

Forums and Social Media Groups

While formal education is crucial, never underestimate the power of a good online community. Websites like Reddit's Machine Learning community, Stack Overflow, and specialized LinkedIn Groups offer the chance to engage with like-minded individuals. These are places where you can ask questions, share resources, learn about the latest advancements, and even find mentors.

Books and Research Papers

Books like "Superintelligence" by Nick Bostrom or "Life 3.0" by Max Tegmark offer philosophical insights into the implications of AI. For technical learning, "The Hundred-Page Machine Learning Book" by Andriy

Burkov is highly recommended. Platforms like Google Scholar, ResearchGate, and arXiv offer a wealth of peer-reviewed papers on AI topics.

Bootcamps and Workshops

Many institutions and organizations offer bootcamps and workshops that provide hands-on experience in AI. These are excellent for gaining practical knowledge and networking with professionals in the field.

MOOCs (Massive Open Online Courses)

Websites like Khan Academy, and even YouTube, provide free courses on AI. While these might not offer the depth that some of the paid courses provide, they're an excellent starting point for beginners.

GitHub Repositories

For those who want to dive right into the code, GitHub is a fantastic resource. You can find a myriad of AI projects, ranging from beginner to expert levels. Many professionals share their work openly, providing an invaluable real-world educational resource.

Peer-to-Peer Learning

As the African proverb goes, "If you want to go fast, go alone. If you want to go far, go together." Engaging with a community doesn't just provide learning opportunities; it offers a chance for you to share your knowledge and learn through teaching. The ability to articulate complex ideas in simple terms is a skill that will serve you well, especially in a field as complex as AI.

Endnote: The Journey Towards Mastery

As we embark on our AI literacy journey, let's remember that mastery is more about the journey than the destination. AI literacy is less about becoming an encyclopedia of all things AI, and more about developing the critical thinking skills, technical prowess, and ethical considerations that will make you an effective participant in this new world.
By sharing our wins and losses and collaborating with a global community, we're not just adding a new skill to our individual portfolios; we're contributing to a collective body of knowledge, an evolving narrative that will shape our future as a society. So go ahead, dive into these resources, keep your eyes open, and remember—every day is a school day.

Concluding Thoughts - When Hope Drives You

In a landscape as vast and rapidly evolving as artificial intelligence, it's easy to feel daunted. The sheer volume of information, the complexities of the algorithms, the ethical implications—all these elements can, understandably, instill a sense of trepidation. But let's not lose sight of something indispensable: hope.

The tale of human progress has always been a story of overcoming challenges, from harnessing fire to landing on the moon. The story of AI should not be any different. When hope drives you, acquiring new skills isn't a burden but an adventure—a thrilling narrative in which you are both the protagonist and the narrator.

Remember, we're at the forefront of a new era. We're not just passive bystanders but active participants shaping a future with unprecedented tools at our disposal. And while the tools are complex, our mission is profoundly human: to make our lives and the lives of those around us better, more meaningful, and more enriched.

In a world where we can summon cars with the tap of a screen, where we can speak to someone halfway around the world in real-time, where we can unravel the mysteries of DNA and peer into the far reaches of the universe, how can we not be hopeful? How can we not be excited about the transformative potential of AI?

As you close this chapter and consider diving into the educational resources laid out before you, let hope be your guiding star. Let it lead you through the labyrinthine complexities of neural networks, the challenging algorithms of machine learning, and the ethical mazes of data usage. Let hope spur you into action, into learning, into becoming a part of this extraordinary epoch in human history.

So, when you find yourself knee-deep in codes you don't understand or grappling with concepts that seem beyond your grasp, let your hope refocus your lens. For every challenge you face, there's an equally great—or greater—opportunity. And each obstacle is not a dead-end but a stepping stone on your adventure through the captivating world of AI.

Yes, there's much to learn, but there's even more to hope for. Your individual journey in understanding and mastering AI could well be a microcosm of humanity's collective journey toward a better future. We're all in this together, shaping, learning, creating. And as long as hope drives us, the horizon will always be bright.

Chapter 8: The Human-AI Symbiosis: Philosophical and Ethical Considerations

The relationship between humans and AI isn't just a practical one; it also invites philosophical and ethical inquiries that have fascinated thinkers for generations. To broach these complex topics, let's entertain a somewhat speculative—yet not entirely implausible— idea: What if the story of humanity, its triumphs and failures, its moral zeniths and nadirs, is akin to a divine algorithm, an existential form of AI?

It's a fanciful notion, one more commonly explored in the realms of fiction or theology, but it serves as a useful metaphor for our present discussion. Imagine a

Creator, coding "generations" as complex algorithms, each designed with specific variables—ethics, ambition, societal structures, and even flaws. If the program doesn't run as anticipated, it's back to the drawing board, or in divine terms, a "regeneration."

Consider, for example, the Greatest Generation—those who lived through the Great Depression and fought in World War II. A generation that endured hardships, that fostered unity and resilience, and that built systems and institutions aimed at global peace and economic stability. In a way, it was like a program that ran extraordinarily well, hitting almost all the expected outcomes.

Then came the Silent Generation, preceded by such a monumental "update" that it would be hard for any successor to match. It was a generation that grew up in the shadow of war and economic instability but didn't face the same urgent calls to collective action. Instead, this period was marked by a kind of moral and ethical "coding error," one that produced a society rife with deep-rooted prejudices, rigid gender roles, and a dangerous complacency in the face of civil injustices. Women were limited to domestic spheres, confined by patriarchal norms, and discrimination based on race, gender, and class was rampant.

Consequently, the next "iteration" in this human algorithm—the Baby Boomers—found themselves predisposed to challenge these existing codes. They became the rebels, the hippies, the civil rights activists; they aimed to debug the system, so to speak. Fueled by revolutionary zeal, they sought peace, love, and above all, drastic societal reform.

Now, let's pivot this analogy back to our coexistence with AI, which brings its own share of philosophical and ethical quandaries. One immediate question that arises is: To what extent should we let AI rewrite our societal, moral, or even existential "codes"? How far should we allow machine algorithms to influence or even determine human behavior, ethics, or justice? Imagine AI systems so advanced they can predict criminal activity before it happens, á la "Minority Report." Such a capability begs the question: Is it ethical to arrest someone based on a future crime they have not yet committed? Or take AI in healthcare, where algorithms can predict potential future illnesses. Should insurance companies have access to this information? Would it be ethical for them to alter premiums based on this data?

And here's another ethical labyrinth: AI's role in shaping public opinion. If AI algorithms can understand human psychology well enough to predict and even manipulate behavior (think social media feeds), what ethical boundaries should be put in place? Do we risk creating a society not of free will but of "programmed" citizens?

The consideration extends to autonomy and identity, too. If AI can perform most of our tasks, from the menial to the complex, where does that leave human uniqueness? What aspects of "being human" should never be outsourced to algorithms, no matter how advanced?

In grappling with these questions, one point becomes abundantly clear: The ethics of AI are intrinsically linked with human ethics. Just as we've iterated through generations, learning from our collective mistakes and triumphs, so too must we iterate through versions of AI, debugging as we go along.

It's an endeavor that calls for ongoing scrutiny, for moral and philosophical debates as robust as the codes that power the algorithms. As we continue to advance in this brave new world of AI, we have an ethical responsibility to ensure that these technologies are being coded in a way that aligns with our highest ideals.

Because, at the end of the day, the AI algorithms we create are reflections of ourselves—our morals, our values, our flaws. We are the "programmers" in this grand project, and the script we write will, for better or worse, dictate the future of human-AI symbiosis.

So, as we stand on this precipice, looking out into the uncharted territories that AI will undoubtedly explore, let us proceed with caution but also with a sense of moral duty. For in our hands lies not just code, but the very essence of what it means to be human.

The Role of Emotional Intelligence and Collective Wisdom

The ancient African proverb, "If you want to go fast, go by yourself. If you want to go far, go with others," serves as an insightful addition to our dialogue on the human-AI symbiosis. It captures an essential element that's often overlooked in the mad rush to be 'first' in this digital age—collective wisdom. The seduction of speed and novelty often blinds us to the multidimensional challenges and the wealth of nuanced understanding required to navigate the complexities of AI ethically and effectively.

Today, we find no shortage of self-proclaimed "AI experts" and "AI gurus" eager to offer up bite-sized courses that promise to transform you into an AI prodigy overnight. These are often the swiftest swimmers who've barely gotten their feet wet but are already peddling their early splashes as profound dives into an ocean they've scarcely surveyed.

The proverbial Atlantis that lies beneath the surface is, in fact, an ecosystem of profound algorithms, ethical dilemmas, and technological capabilities that can either uplift humanity or contribute to its degradation. Skimming the surface might offer some the thrill of speed, the immediate rewards of being first to market, but it can never provide the sustainable, long-lasting benefits that can only be garnered from deep, collective exploration.

This is where the concept of emotional intelligence (EQ) enters the discussion. EQ—the ability to understand, interpret, and respond to human emotions—serves as a form of intellectual richness that machines, at least for the foreseeable future, can't replicate. It involves self-awareness, empathy, social skills, and emotional regulation—qualities that are quintessentially human and deeply necessary for ethical decision-making and communal well-being.

In the context of AI, emotional intelligence plays a crucial role in understanding the human side of technology. It helps us navigate the ethical gray areas, build algorithms that are sensitive to human needs, and create AI applications that complement rather than combat human faculties. Furthermore, EQ is invaluable in team settings, where diverse perspectives must be harmonized to drive innovation and ensure ethical compliance. It acts as the adhesive in multi-disciplinary teams, enabling computer scientists, ethicists, psychologists, and other professionals to collaborate more effectively.

The emotionally intelligent approach also helps in countering "Real Ignorance"—a term that encapsulates not only a lack of knowledge but also a lack of curiosity and empathy. By appreciating the depths and not just the shallows, by seeking to go far and not just fast, emotionally intelligent individuals contribute to a form of collective wisdom. They resist the impulse to monetize every early understanding, recognizing that such actions could lead to misinformation and, ultimately, societal harm.

Remember, those who are trapped in the quest to churn out doggy-paddle coursework on AI might gain immediate gratification but will inevitably miss the deeper revelations. Their pursuit of speed and novelty can often come at the expense of true understanding and ethical considerations, locking them in a cycle that leaves little room for depth or collaborative growth.

So, as we deepen our journey into the world of AI, let us recognize the importance of emotional intelligence and the wisdom of collective endeavor. These are not mere supplements to technical know-how; they are fundamental components of a balanced, ethical, and sustainable relationship with technology.

In other words, AI's full potential can only be realized through a symbiotic relationship between machine intelligence and human emotional intelligence, between going fast and going far. For the true power of AI doesn't lie in its ability to outthink us, but in its capacity, when ethically applied, to help us become the best versions of ourselves—more understanding, more empathetic, and more profoundly human.

Concluding Thoughts: Navigating the Inevitable

Bill Gates's proclamation in the mid-1990s that "If your business is not on the internet, then your business will be out of business" seems almost prescient now. At the time he made that statement, it was far from an accepted truth. The internet was still in its fledgling state, unfamiliar to the masses, and represented only a tiny fraction of the business landscape.
Fast forward to today, and the internet is not merely a business tool; it is the business environment.

Much like the early days of the internet, we stand at a similar precipice with artificial intelligence. The resistance, the doubts, and the fears parallel those early days of the World Wide Web. Yet, just as businesses had to adapt or perish in the new digital environment, the same rule is gradually, but firmly, becoming true for AI.

Let's be clear: AI is not a threat in the sense of some dystopian future where machines revolt against humanity. The actual threat lies in the ignorance of not adopting, or at least understanding, the transformative power of AI. In that sense, it isn't AI that will replace your job; it's the person who understood AI's capabilities and adapted accordingly who will. They will be the new hires, the new leaders, the new entrepreneurs of an increasingly AI-driven world.

Today, the quaint storefronts of yesteryears have migrated into digital domains, hosted on servers and accessible by a click. Similarly, the quaint notions of doing business—relying solely on human effort without the augmentation of intelligent systems—are undergoing a seismic shift. Businesses of the future will either be adept at leveraging AI, or they will increasingly find themselves unable to compete. It's not a scare tactic; it's an observation grounded in the trajectory of technological evolution.

In a decade, the landscape will likely bifurcate into businesses that have effectively integrated AI into their models and those struggling to catch up. The latter, unfortunately, may find themselves fading into obsolescence, just like those businesses that were too slow to adopt the internet.
So, where does that leave you? The choice is less about resisting AI and more about understanding where you fit into this new ecosystem. Will you be among the pioneers, or will you be among those desperately trying to catch up?

The time to decide is now. The world won't wait. AI certainly won't. And perhaps the question isn't whether you can afford to invest in understanding AI, but whether you can afford not to.

Chapter 9: AI in Healthcare and Medicine

Case Studies of AI Being Used for Good

The realm of healthcare and medicine has always been at the forefront of adopting new technologies, out of necessity and the eternal quest to improve the human condition. It's perhaps the most human of all sectors—where lives, not just livelihoods, are at stake. In this vital area, artificial intelligence is already proving to be a game-changer. Let's delve into a few case studies that highlight the transformative power of AI in healthcare and medicine.

Case Study 1: Predictive Analytics in Cardiology

Cardiovascular diseases are among the leading causes of death worldwide. Traditional diagnostics like echocardiograms and stress tests are incredibly valuable but often detect heart issues only after they have reached a critical stage. Enter predictive analytics powered by machine learning. Algorithms are now able to analyze medical images to predict potential heart failures years before they manifest in symptoms.

The idea isn't to replace cardiologists but to empower them. Doctors can combine their expert judgment with predictive insights to offer preventative treatments. Here, AI acts as a second set of "hyper-observant" eyes, processing the minutiae in medical images that might be humanly impossible to dissect at scale.

Case Study 2: Drug Discovery and Development

Creating a new drug is a time-consuming and financially draining process. However, AI algorithms specialized in combing through vast amounts of biomedical literature, clinical studies, and molecular data can predict how different drugs will interact with targets in the body. This significantly shortens the drug development lifecycle.

A case in point is the rapid development of vaccines for COVID-19. Machine learning algorithms sorted through an ocean of viral protein structures to identify potential points of attack, enabling scientists to design more effective vaccines faster than ever before.

Case Study 3: Mental Health Monitoring

The challenge with mental health is that it's often subjective, relying on patient reporting. However, AI tools are becoming increasingly sophisticated at gauging psychological well-being. For instance, natural language processing can analyze text and spoken words for signs of mental distress. While not a substitute for professional medical advice, such AI systems can act as early warning systems, flagging at-risk individuals for further evaluation.

Case Study 4: Remote Monitoring and Telehealth

The COVID-19 pandemic accelerated the adoption of telehealth services, and AI has a significant role in this. Wearable devices equipped with AI algorithms can continuously monitor vital statistics, relaying information in real-time to healthcare providers. This not only makes healthcare more accessible but also allows for timely interventions before a health crisis escalates.

Case Study 5: AI in Oncology

Cancer remains one of the most researched yet least understood of medical conditions. Machine learning models trained to analyze complex patterns in genetic mutations, lifestyle factors, and even social determinants are making strides in predicting cancer susceptibility. In treatment, AI can assist oncologists by analyzing the cellular structure of tumors, comparing them against vast databases of cancer images, and recommending a course of action based on the most similar cases.

These examples barely scratch the surface, but they illuminate the profound impacts AI can have on healthcare and medicine. Whether it's by saving time or saving lives, AI is an invaluable tool in the relentless pursuit of wellness. Rather than seeing AI as an abstract, nebulous force, these case studies help us ground its applications in tangible, life-altering ways.

The promise is not just in solving abstract problems, but in elevating the quality of human life.

What these case studies manifestly show is that AI is far from being the doom-and-gloom machinery of job loss and impersonality. In the right hands, focused through the lens of human ingenuity and ethical responsibility, it's a technology that holds the potential to revolutionize not just how we live, but how well we live.

Let this sink in: Artificial Intelligence can be, and already is, a force for undeniable good. It's up to us to guide its path moving forward.

The Potential Pitfalls and Ethical Considerations

While the advancements in AI in healthcare are awe-inspiring and transformative, the road ahead isn't without its bumps. As we integrate AI further into our medical infrastructure, we need to be hyper-aware of the ethical and practical challenges that come with it. In healthcare, even the smallest error can have dire consequences. Therefore, let's shed light on the darker corners where we need to tread carefully.

Data Privacy

In healthcare, AI often operates on extremely sensitive data—everything from your medical history to your DNA. While this data is essential for the kind of analytics AI performs, its misuse could lead to egregious violations of privacy. Imagine insurance companies accessing this data and using it to deny coverage or increase premiums. Ethical considerations about who gets access to what data and for what purpose need to be codified into law.

Bias in Algorithms

AI is only as good as the data it's trained on. If the training data is biased, the AI will be too. For example, an AI model trained predominantly on data from a particular ethnic group may perform poorly for people from other ethnicities. This is not just a question of algorithmic accuracy; it's an issue of social justice and equality.

The "Black Box" Problem

One of the biggest criticisms against AI in healthcare is the opaqueness of complex algorithms. If a machine learning model recommends a certain treatment or diagnoses a condition, medical practitioners want to know why. The inability to "open the black box" and understand the rationale behind decisions could be a hurdle in gaining clinicians' trust.

Accessibility

As AI tools become more sophisticated, there's the issue of accessibility. Advanced healthcare technologies tend to be expensive and may not be easily available in resource-poor settings. This creates a risk of widening the healthcare gap between affluent and impoverished communities, both within nations and between them.

Dehumanization of Care

While AI can handle data and analytics well, it cannot replace the human touch in healthcare. From empathetic communication to nuanced decision-making based on a patient's unique situation, healthcare is deeply personal. There's a valid concern that over-reliance on AI could make healthcare feel impersonal and mechanized, eroding the doctor-patient relationship that is fundamental to good care.

Liability and Accountability

Who is responsible if an AI-powered diagnostic tool makes an error? Is it the healthcare provider, the software developer, or the machine learning model itself? As AI gains a more prominent role in patient care, the legal and ethical frameworks around liability and accountability need to be solidified.

The Ethical Debate on AI-Generated Treatment Plans

The use of AI in developing treatment plans—particularly in terminal cases—opens a Pandora's Box of ethical questions. For example, should AI be allowed to suggest cessation of treatment for a terminally ill patient based on statistical improbability of recovery? Where do we draw the line on what AI should and should not be allowed to decide?

While AI has the potential to revolutionize healthcare, these challenges and ethical considerations must be addressed with rigorous oversight, clear legislation, and a moral code that puts the welfare of human beings above all else. By doing so, we won't just be implementing technology; we'll be elevating healthcare to new ethical and effective standards.

It's imperative for everyone, from policymakers to healthcare providers, to be aware of both the incredible potential and the ethical pitfalls of AI in healthcare. For in our hands lies the power to shape a tool of immense potential—either as a boon for humanity or, if we're not careful, a bane.

Personal Narration: The Miracle of Modern Healthcare Solutions, Thanks to AI

Allow me to tell you a story, one that's particularly close to my heart, about how AI transformed not just an outcome, but an entire life.

My son's friend was diagnosed with a rare form of leukemia at the age of 4. He underwent the usual course of treatment—chemotherapy, medication, frequent hospital visits—but his condition showed minimal improvement. The physicians were baffled and disheartened; they had exhausted the resources of their traditional medical knowledge.

Then, enter AI. His medical team decided to use a machine learning model that had been trained on various kinds of leukemia treatments from across the globe. This AI had processed information from thousands of similar cases, learned from the outcomes, and was able to predict with a remarkable degree of accuracy which treatment combinations were most likely to succeed. The AI suggested a course of treatment that had never been considered for the child—a mix of two drugs that were rarely used together but had shown promise in similar cases.

It was a shot in the dark, but a calculated one. And it worked. Within months, his condition improved dramatically. She went from having a few months to live to a realistic prospect of remission. Today, she is back at work, planning for a future she thought she'd lost.

What happened with Sarah is not isolated. Across the world, AI is making these little miracles possible. It's creating treatment plans for rare diseases, helping surgeons perform complex surgeries with robotic precision, and even predicting outbreaks before they happen. But Sarah's story serves as a poignant reminder that at the core of all this technology, all these algorithms and data points, are real human stories. Stories of suffering, hope, and the unyielding desire to live a better life.

It's not an overstatement to say that AI saved Sarah's life. But beyond that, it saved her family from heartbreak, it saved her friends from loss, and it gave her back her dreams and aspirations. Sarah's experience encapsulates the miracle of modern healthcare solutions, enabled by AI: a lifeline when all other ropes have frayed and snapped.

As we ponder the ethical and practical dimensions of AI in healthcare, let's not lose sight of the ultimate goal: to alleviate suffering and to extend human life in a meaningful way. But to ensure that AI serves us well, we must be its conscientious stewards, addressing the ethical dilemmas and challenges it presents with the same rigor that we apply to its technological development.

So, as we forge ahead into this promising yet complex frontier, let's carry with us the awareness that the choices we make will directly impact lives. The cautionary tales should not deter us but should make us cautious optimists, ever vigilant but always hopeful.

AI, in its essence, is neither good nor bad—it is a tool. And like any tool, its impact depends on the hands that wield it. In Sarah's case, it was wielded wisely, illuminating a path out of despair. Her story gives me hope that we're heading in the right direction, and it reassures me that the miracles of tomorrow are within our grasp today.

Still, the stability of humanity is directly reliant upon the stability of the hands that wield the tools AI introduces into our advancement.

Chapter 10: The Future of AI

In an era teeming with rapid technological evolution, the question is not whether AI will play a central role in our future, but how it will reshape our world in the years to come. In this chapter, we will venture into the speculative yet thrilling territory of what AI could bring us in the next 10, 20, and even 50 years. We'll also delve into the ethical maelstrom that comes with it and round off with a personal reflection on the responsibilities we bear as creators and consumers of this groundbreaking technology.

Speculative Projections for the Next 10, 20, 50 Years

The Next 10 Years

In the short term, we're likely to see AI becoming a staple in healthcare, as we discussed in the previous chapter. We can expect machine learning models to become more sophisticated, offering personalized treatment options. Smart cities will finally move from being a lofty idea to a livable reality, with AI systems managing everything from traffic flow to waste management.

The Next 20 Years

As we venture two decades into the future, we might see AI integrated into our legal systems, helping judges make more informed decisions by analyzing historical cases and perhaps even predicting the societal impact of their judgments. In education, AI could offer personalized learning experiences tailored to each student's pace and style of learning.

The Next 50 Years

Fifty years from now, we enter the realm of science fiction turning into science fact. We might encounter AI that not only replicates human intelligence but also understands and mimics human emotions—artificial emotional intelligence, if you will. The boundary between man and machine could become increasingly blurred, leading us to question the very nature of consciousness and identity.

Ethical Concerns: Surveillance, Decision-Making, Etc.

When we think of the future, we often focus on the gleaming possibilities, the revolutionary advancements, and the problems that technology can solve. Yet, the ethical landscape that AI brings is complex and replete with both pitfalls and paradoxes. While AI promises to make our lives easier, safer, and more efficient, it simultaneously raises ethical concerns about surveillance, decision-making, and the very essence of human agency. This ethical complexity isn't a detour on the road to progress; it's part of the very path itself. To navigate it wisely, we need to dissect these ethical concerns in greater detail.

The Surveillance State: From Convenience to Control

In today's world, it's already common to have smart cameras equipped with facial recognition at airports, railway stations, and even on our doorsteps. We've largely accepted these as conveniences that add a layer of security to our lives. But what happens when such surveillance becomes pervasive, ceaselessly watching, and predicting not just our movements but also our potential actions?

The idea of predictive policing—where AI could forecast criminal behavior before it happens—has echoes of dystopian fiction like "Minority Report." On one hand, it promises a safer world where crimes can be stopped before they occur. On the other hand, it flirts dangerously with civil liberties. If AI systems are monitoring our online conversations, analyzing our social patterns, and predicting our future actions, what room is left for privacy or free will? We risk crossing the line from a democracy into an Orwellian state where "Big Brother is watching you," not to serve you better ads but to predict—and maybe even control—your next move.

Decision-Making: When AI Chooses Who Lives and Who Dies

The ethical conundrums become even more acute when AI systems make life-or-death decisions. Consider self-driving cars. These vehicles use AI algorithms to interpret the world around them and make driving decisions in real-time. In an emergency, an AI might have to decide whether to swerve into a barrier, potentially harming the passenger, or hit a pedestrian who has suddenly appeared in its path.

The underlying moral dilemma has been a topic of debate for ethicists long before AI came into the picture—the infamous "trolley problem." But while in philosophy, it remains a theoretical dilemma, AI has the potential to make it all too real. Who gets to program the moral code into an AI? How can these choices be democratic and represent societal values, and not just the perspectives of a team of engineers?

The Conundrum of Medical Ethics

AI has made remarkable strides in the field of healthcare, offering the potential for personalized medicine and rapid diagnostics. However, there is an ethical minefield to navigate here as well. AI algorithms could predict the likelihood of a patient's survival and could thus influence decisions about who receives treatment in a resource-constrained setting like an intensive care unit. The AI may choose to allocate resources to those most likely to survive, but what does that mean for the ethics of healthcare, which traditionally has aimed to save every life, regardless of the odds?

The Multiplicity of Ethical Dilemmas

As AI technologies become more complex, the ethical challenges they present will likely multiply rather than diminish. From deepfake technologies that can convincingly replace reality, to AI in warfare that can choose targets autonomously, we are entering an era where algorithms can make decisions that were traditionally the sole purview of human judgment.

How do we safeguard human agency and ethical values in this landscape? How do we ensure that these technologies are designed and used in a way that respects human dignity, freedom, and equality? These are questions that require not just technological expertise, but also a deep engagement with ethics, philosophy, and social sciences.

Ethical concerns in AI are not hypothetical, distant issues; they are immediate and pressing. As AI becomes increasingly integrated into our daily lives, our legal systems, our economies, and our social fabric, it becomes imperative to actively engage with these ethical dimensions. It's not just about preventing a dystopian future; it's about shaping an ethical, equitable, and just world that we can all inhabit. Ignoring these concerns would be, in essence, programming our future for ethical failure. Therefore, as we marvel at the scientific miracles that AI promises, we must also arm ourselves with ethical frameworks that help us navigate this brave, new, complex world.

Personal Note: Taking Responsibility for the World We're Creating, Ensuring it Aligns with Our Values

So, here we are, on the cusp of perhaps the most significant technological revolution humanity has ever seen. We wield an immense power, but as the age-old adage goes, "With great power comes great responsibility." We are the architects of this new world, and it's upon us to ensure that the society we're building aligns with our collective values.

It's easy to relegate the responsibility to tech companies, governments, or some nebulous "other," but the reality is that we are all stakeholders in this. Just as we vote with our ballots, we also vote with our data, our attention, and our wallets. Every product we use, every app we download, every service we enjoy contributes to the world that AI will create.

Therefore, it's incumbent upon us to be educated, informed citizens of this brave new world. We need to learn enough to ask the right questions, to hold the decision-makers accountable, and to make ethical choices ourselves, both as consumers and potential creators of AI technologies

In summation, AI is a mirror that reflects the best and worst of who we are. It can amplify our most enlightened ideas and our darkest impulses. Its trajectory is not predestined but is a path that we carve out through our choices. The future is not a passive destination waiting for us at the end of a road but is being actively built, one algorithm, one line of code, and one ethical decision at a time. Let us build it wisely.

Chapter 11: The Alpha in the Age of AI - Embracing an Alpha Mentality in a World Dictated by Data

This chapter touches particularly close to home for me. I've often been described as an "alpha," a label that simultaneously conjures respect and ignites debates. As a high-ranking C-level employee in a male-dominated industry--and, separately, a burgeoning new business owner, I occupy spaces that are steeped in tradition, hierarchy, and set patterns of thinking. While I wouldn't necessarily describe myself as a true iconoclast, I do find myself turning tradition on its heels in some critical ways. So how does one navigate an alpha mentality in a world increasingly dictated by data, algorithms, and machine-driven decision-making? This is what we'll explore in this chapter.

Being an alpha in this age of AI doesn't mean resisting technological progress or sidelining the power of data. Rather, it's about understanding these tools deeply and leveraging them to augment one's leadership style. The alpha personality is often associated with leadership, drive, ambition, and the ability to influence and direct scenarios and people. In the era of AI, these traits aren't becoming obsolete; they're becoming more crucial but in a nuanced way.

Traditionally, being an alpha meant exerting control, often in a top-down manner. The rapid rise of AI and data analytics is changing this dynamic. As a leader in today's world, one must understand the complexity and potential of data-driven insights. An alpha in the AI era knows how to ask the right questions, scrutinize data critically, and use it to make informed decisions. They don't shy away from rolling up their sleeves and diving into the analytics dashboard; instead, they embrace it as another tool for effective leadership.

But this is not just about being data-savvy; it's about integrating emotional intelligence and ethical considerations into one's leadership style. AI can provide us with unparalleled insights into human behavior, predicting outcomes based on intricate algorithms. Still, it can't replace the human traits of empathy, moral reasoning, and the ability to inspire and motivate. An alpha leader recognizes this gap and fills it, forming a symbiotic relationship with AI tools rather than viewing them as a threat or a replacement.

This form of leadership also demands a greater degree of adaptability and lifelong learning. The pace at which AI and machine learning technologies are advancing requires an alpha to be on the constant lookout for new trends, understand their impact, and pivot strategies accordingly. Stagnation is the antithesis of the alpha mentality, especially in this rapidly evolving landscape.
As AI becomes increasingly entrenched in organizational structures, workflows, and decision-making processes, the alpha leader also bears the

ethical responsibility to ensure these technologies are deployed fairly and judiciously. This entails grappling with complex issues, from data privacy and surveillance to ensuring algorithms don't perpetuate existing social inequalities.

So, as we find ourselves standing at the intersection of leadership traits and artificial intelligence, let's make it clear: being an alpha in this landscape is not just about maintaining the status quo in a new setting. It's about transforming the very essence of what it means to lead, to influence, and to forge paths in a world where the trails are often blazed by algorithms. Being an alpha in the age of AI means mastering the art of harmonizing human intuition with machine intelligence, ethical considerations with data-driven decision-making, and individual ambition with collective well-being. It's a complex, challenging, yet exhilarating task—and one that I, for one, am keen to embrace.

The Difference Between Being an Alpha and a Narcissist in the AI Age

Navigating the complexities of human behavior and relationships in the AI age is like walking a tightrope. While the label of "alpha" often gets bandied about in discussions around leadership and assertiveness, another term also frequently makes its appearance: narcissist. Though some people conflate the two, they are distinct, and understanding this difference is crucial for personal and professional development in a world increasingly run by algorithms.

Let's start by considering the psychological underpinnings of narcissism. Narcissistic Personality Disorder, a clinical diagnosis, involves a long-term pattern of exaggerated self-importance, the need for excessive attention, and a lack of empathy for others. This psychological trait can lead to toxic environments, whether in the corporate world or personal relationships.

On a related note, it's interesting how the label of "narcissist" gets thrown around, often by individuals who perceive themselves as victims in a relationship where their love or interest isn't reciprocated. While the pain of unrequited love is real, it's essential to differentiate between genuine narcissism and a situation where one party is merely uninterested or unable to commit. Labeling someone as a narcissist in such instances can sometimes reflect more on the person making the accusation than on the accused.

Contrast this with an alpha mentality, which I cultivated through situational circumstances that forced me to trust my instincts and continually seek improvement. In my journey, Pinnacle Sales Coaching played an instrumental role. After experiencing a setback with a failed agency and finding myself in a $50k-a-year marketing and sales position, I used their services to elevate myself. I've transitioned from that relatively modest role to becoming a C-level employee, an entrepreneur, and a non-profit founder, with a future brighter than I ever imagined.

In speaking with my coach regarding this book, we discussed how AI assists in the expansion of your own thoughts, forcing you to delve deeper and conceptualize greater at times, and how it still takes the human touch to create. In as much as my Catholic upbringing taught me, we may be able to clone a man, but without the breath of the Holy Spirit, it will have no grasp of right or wrong. While we have cloned physical bodies, AI is the cloning of the mind, and without the breath, and the touch of humanity, it cannot exist to govern right and wrong.

In the same way, Tim Scholze, the founder at Pinnacle coached me, it is a domino effect, a contagion that begins with a thought. He pushed me and as I learned and leaned and fell forward in the process, a contagion happened. Momentum picked up, growth happened and here I am, pushing AI to continue that contagion. Where did it begin?

Being an alpha isn't about superiority or denigrating others to uplift oneself. It's about setting your internal "bar" high, continually striving for growth, and surrounding yourself with individuals smarter than you. An alpha takes what life offers not as a threat but as an opportunity—a lifeline if you will. They also possess the savvy to sidestep the traps set by the unscrupulous who are out to make a quick buck, especially critical in an era where AI and data can be manipulated to serve nefarious ends.

In the following section, I will delve into some deeply personal experiences that shaped me into who I am today. These stories are testaments to how one can rise, accept opportunities as they come, and continuously strive for personal and collective betterment. It's a testament to how the true alpha mentality can help you navigate a landscape that is as promising as it is perilous, particularly in this AI-driven age.

Personal Affirmation: Guarding and Feeding Your Internal Sense of Hope and Ambition in an AI-Driven World

Life's journey is rarely a straight path; it is instead a tapestry of experiences that shape who we are and inform our future. As we stand at the precipice of a world increasingly governed by AI and data, our internal compass—our hope, ambition, and sense of self—becomes more vital than ever. In this complicated terrain, where algorithms can often eclipse human interaction, guarding your internal flame becomes a form of resistance and a source of power.

I've chosen to share a piece of this internal journey with you—a chapter from a memoir I'm currently writing, which will be published in the near future. If you find yourself intrigued by this glimpse into my life, I invite you to explore the full nonfiction biography upon its release.

Excerpts from the chapter, titled "Fire, Suspended," is more than a narrative; it serves as a metaphor for the tenacity and resilience required to navigate our rapidly changing world. In an era where your job, your relationships, and even your self-worth could be quantified by machine intelligence, insights from personal experiences can be your anchor.

Now, without further ado, let me take you through this somewhat abridged, yet still intimate chapter of my life. It's a piece that I hold close to my heart, and I believe its messages will resonate with anyone who aims to safeguard their inner fire in this age of AI.

Fire, Suspended

My twenties were a decade I rarely look back on with any depth. If I go beyond some superficial pleasant times, the worst of times lurk in my memory, much further down, in shady recesses I am fortunate remain vague now. My father died when I was 19. I subtly derailed, bit-by-gradual-bit. My friend Tate often tells me now, you just have that something about you that drives men crazy. He doesn't know what an understatement that has seemed to be in the lifetime that occurred between 19 and now. And how very much that has served not as a blessing, but as a curse.

In 2008, after being assumed dead, which was the only way I escaped alive by the man I was casually dating, I packed up and moved in the dark of night to a lake town in far north Texas, on the border of Oklahoma. The two states were separated by the expansive Texoma River, the Red River, as it was known to locals. I worked remotely, so I didn't think it would matter much where I moved, and this rural spot seemed safe and picturesque. It felt like an ideal hiding place where I could slowly heal, physically and emotionally. Then the economy took a nosedive and a company bought out the one I worked for, letting go all of the remote employees. I didn't know what I would do and there were no decent jobs around.

So a bleached-blonde, fake-tanned, former or possibly-current, crack-smoking neighbor with large fake breasts always popping out of ridiculously small tops and a large belly popping out of ridiculously low-cut and equally as tight jeans, recommended I try to get a job at a local bar. She sized me up and said my looks and the "size of my chest" would definitely make me good money.

One day, a cow barber I'd befriended...yes, it's a thing in southern rural towns, took me to a local watering hole on the Oklahoma side and introduced me to the owner, Coyote Dan. He took one look at me and despite my never having made a drink and not having a license to, asked me when I could start.

After a month or two of slinging drinks, I had my own fan following of local cowboys and hustling pool sharks. I still possessed a residual discomfort around men, given how the last relationship had ended up. Until recently, I had not even been able to feel comfortable alone in the same room with the opposite sex. Now here I was, making drinks and poised on display on a man's favorite pedestal (that is behind the bar), feeling a bit like a daycare worker, breaking up fights, cleaning up bathroom accidents, putting bottles in mouths of crying babes, and letting one or two get a much needed nap in, right there where their head fell to rest on the table.

Monday was Men's Day at Coyote Dan's bar. The other girls said it was the coveted day to work. Monday was the money maker. Only men were allowed in on Monday, and they would pay the bartender handsomely to basically flirt religiously. Rather than give my morals the day off, I took Mondays off.

Then like every good country story, something tragic happened that put me in a huge *pickle*.

I was out with my two dogs on an afternoon off. I took them to a graveyard to run and stretch because it was fenced and because, well, I love graveyards. This little white dog with spots, named Rascal, found her way out of the gate and across the road winding by the graveyard. I called for her to *get back right now*, which, for the first time in Rascal's life, she decided to heed me and turned and came sprinting back across the road to me with such a look of obedient joy, her tongue lolling and tail wagging. That was when I saw the family van coming down the road rather speedily. Though the owner tried to avoid it, she hit Rascal with her front tire and pulled over to help, crying and apologizing.

I got the bloody, whimpering dog to a nearby vet and they said she may be saved by having her hind leg amputated or a metal rod put in. It was shattered. The metal rod approach had no guarantee of healing properly and was thousands more than I could afford-- or, I could just put the dog down, they suggested, as that would be far more cost-effective.

As I stood there in the office considering my options, a woman came in with a dog she boasted had been on Oprah. The dog was named "Faith" and had been born with a defect where it only had hind legs and walked upright and laid down very carefully but seemed very happy. I decided it was a sign and I should amputate the one injured leg of Rascal's. Afterall, she had three more, so she was better off than poor Faith. However, I still needed a fair amount of money I didn't have for the procedure.

Suddenly, the fact that it was Monday occurred to me. What was of greater importance? My sense of pride in the honest work I did, or getting the money I needed to help Rascal? I could do it, right?

Back in Oklahoma and several lifetimes later, the men at Coyote Dan's knew I was aware of what was expected on Mondays and they knew I had said I would never work a Monday. So when I walked in that night, the money started piling in the tip jars. Big bills. Easily enough to pay for the surgery several times. Talk about PTSD coming on strong, I was the only female in the entire establishment.

Coyote Dan could see I was off my game and anxious and seemed to take me under his wing, telling the men to leave me alone and go back to their business. When the night wrapped, I was exhausted and it was storming outside. I got in the car and wanted to hurry away as fast as I could.

I ran through the pouring rain got in my car and sped out of that parking lot and into the night, trying to make my way back to Texas. The roads were winding and hilly and there was no cell signal at all. Suddenly some animal ran out in front of my car and thinking of Rascal, I tried to swerve to the right and lost control, spinning across the road and slamming headfirst into a tree.
My airbags deployed. I got out of the car quickly and grabbed my phone, trying to see if I could call for help. Still no signal. In front of me were miles and miles of country backroad with no open businesses or houses on it, and pouring rain. The only open establishment nearby was Coyote Dan's, which meant that I had to backtrack on foot to the place I had just run left in exhaustion.

So I started walking along the side of the country road and it wasn't long before headlights pierced through the night rain in front of me. I could hear country music and voices. They passed me and brake lights lit up red in the darkness as the truck slid into reverse and passed me again. It then moved back into drive and turned toward me as if to provide some light for me, and to better see me. Only the lights were too close and I couldn't see, so I tried to shield my eyes. The only thing is, the truck didn't stop, it was speeding up on its approach and the lights were at once closer and brighter. The force of it slamming into me was hard enough to throw me horizontally into the air where I was caught by the barbed-wire fence and pinned by the honeycomb grill of the truck. The truck then came to a stop, but the pressure seemed to slowly intensify against my face and body, and I realized I would be decapitated if the driver allowed it to roll even a bit further. I had barbed wire running along my neck, my ribs and my ankles.

I heard female and male voices, the female let out a shrill laugh. They were talking conspiratorially but excitedly, it seemed, too. I called out, begging for my life. Finally, as seconds seemed to turn to minutes, I found myself just wailing aloud to my daddy.
Daddy, please help me. Daddy, *please.*

A male came around the truck to where I was pinned. I knew instantly that something terrible was about to happen. I remember the heavy footsteps approaching in the rain and mud and seeing a form coming into my vision, leaning around the front of the truck, against the barbed wire, to better assess me. I couldn't see his face.

Suddenly more truck lights came up on the scene, slowing down and a voice called out from the window to the man approaching me. The man retreated quickly to the truck, I heard the door slam and the vehicle peeled out backward in a hurry, releasing me from the barbed-wire trap.

A man got out of a kind of beige nondescript truck and approached me. He was older, but he wore a t-shirt that said FIRE on the back and suspenders over it. He put a blanket around my shoulders and instructed me to sit and keep as calm as I could. All was going to be okay soon. His presence alone was soothing.

I tried to gather my wits. The adrenaline was wearing off and I was fading in and out from exhaustion and alcohol and shock. Soon there were tons of emergency vehicles seeming to surround me. All sides. I found myself sitting in the passenger seat of a cop's car. He was shining lights in my eyes and I heard him say I was drunk. I asked him if they got the truck that pinned me. He said I clearly had no idea what I was talking about, I had wrecked my car just a short-distance away.

I tried to explain and he looked at me as if I was not just drunk, but hysterical and he'd seen it so many times before. I told him to ask the man who rescued me, he could verify what happened. He told me, "Ma'am, I happened upon the scene first, and you were sitting off the road with a blanket wrapped around you, having appeared to have wrecked your car, drunk. There was not a soul with you. You were alone."

Then I saw a dark silhouette approach me in the rain and headlights, while I couldn't see a face, I could tell by the lean, muscular shape and size that it was the deaf guy I was sort of talking to (he was very interested in me and never seemed to leave me alone--so I kind of obliged his company as he did fascinate me and kindled my maternal instinct). He got to the cop car and demanded they let me go. The cop told him he could pick me up in the morning. I was going to a holding cell overnight for drunk driving.

When my friend picked me up the next morning, I was still barefoot, bruised and bloody. Our first stop was the hospital, as every part of me hurt. They did x-rays, found contusions of the ribs but nothing seriously injured and nothing broken. They tended to my various cuts from the barbed wire. They said all should heal nicely and I didn't need stitches.

When they inquired into what happened, I told them I had been involved in a hit and run, and they said they were required to notify the police. The officer who showed up said it was his partner who had taken the report the preceding night and he hated to *quarterback off of his efforts* and he seemed to dismiss my story just as quickly.

Immediately after that I asked my male friend to take me to the spot where I wrecked and he did. Maybe 50 yards away there were my shoes, still caught up, a few feet off the ground, in the bramble around the barbed wire fence, where parts of my blonde hair and blood-soaked white blouse still clung and a distinct impression was left by my body in the wire lines. Additionally, there were heavy tire tracks leading straight to the fence and Luke cried out as he followed them and found a condom still in its wrapper, laying on the ground next to them, as if dropped in a hurry. I took pictures with my cell phone and left. I got a lawyer and nothing ever became of that incident, outside of my receiving a drunk-driving charge in the great state of Oklahoma. I never tended bar, nor set foot again in Coyote Dan's. A few years ago I heard Coyote Dan had died.

I asked my friend why he showed up when he did. It was earlier than I typically got out of work and he never went to my bar. He said he was sleeping in bed and suddenly felt the bed shake, as if someone had slammed a huge fist onto it, and he *heard* my dad's voice booming, "Wendi in trouble. Go to Wendi!" Remember, my friend is profoundly deaf and had never met my dad, but that thought didn't seem to even occur to him when he told me it was my dad who woke him and was the reason he jumped in his truck and headed from Texas to Oklahoma in the middle of the stormy night.

****

Years later, I was working in San Antonio and I got to talking to a client/business owner on the phone who was living in Montana or somewhere very rural like that. He started telling me this story of how he came to do the business he did (I honestly can't remember what business he was in now), but it was because he had been involved in some kind of incident that changed his life. He was on his motorcycle, someone tried to run him off the road and he had a major accident. The offending vehicle took off and left him in the middle of the road. He told me it was going to sound crazy but a man showed up in a truck and helped him, got him away from where he was likely to get hit by a speeding car and kept him calm, wrapping a blanket around him. He said he was in and out of consciousness and when he awoke he was in the hospital and had been for some time. He kept asking everyone how he could get in touch with the man who surely saved his life and waited with him until help arrived. The medical team told him that they didn't understand. According to all reports, when help arrived he was there alone, off the road and had apparently found a blanket to wrap around his shoulders.

I asked him to describe the man. He did. He said he was slim and older and was a bit odd, because he wore suspenders. "He wore suspenders over a t-shirt that said "FIRE" on the back?" I asked.

He was quiet and then asked me how I possibly could have known that.

I trust that you will find inspiration and affirmation in these pages. The experiences that shape us are often the most challenging, yet they are the crucible in which our character is formed. And as you turn back to the world, with its ever-accelerating influx of AI and automation, remember that it's not just about surviving in this new world—it's about thriving, and doing so on your own terms.

Chapter 12: Conclusion and Final Reflections

As we come to the end of this exploration into the world of Artificial Intelligence, it's time to pause and reflect on the landscape we've traversed. We've delved into the history, the mechanics, and the applications. We've assessed its impacts on various sectors, from healthcare to finance. We've probed into the ethical considerations, the promise, and the potential pitfalls. But most importantly, we've looked at the deeply human side of this technological behemoth.

Summarizing the Key Takeaways: AI Is a Tool that Can Either Propel Us or Inhibit Us Based on How We Use It

Like any tool, the utility of AI is determined by the hands that wield it. It can either elevate humanity to new heights or plunge us into the abyss of ethical and societal quandaries. AI has the potential to cure diseases, alleviate poverty, and solve some of our most pressing challenges. Conversely, it can perpetuate inequalities, compromise privacy, and erode human agency. The key takeaway is that AI is not a monolithic entity; it's a complex, dynamic tool that's intimately tied to how we, as a society, decide to employ it.

Final Thoughts: We Are Seeds in This Newly Tilled Ground of Artificial Intelligence; It's Time to Grow

Imagine for a moment that this new era of artificial intelligence is a freshly tilled field. In this metaphor, we are not mere spectators; we are seeds sown into this fertile ground. As seeds, we have within us the capacity to grow and thrive, but only if we actively seek the nutrients that surround us. Those nutrients are the ethical considerations, the wisdom of past experiences, and the embrace of lifelong learning. Like a seed reaches for the sun, so must we reach for knowledge and understanding in this AI-augmented landscape.

Personal Farewell: Straps on Your Boots, Harness the Power of Technology, and Let's Do This. Together.

Before we part ways, I want you to imagine lacing up a pair of shoes—these aren't ordinary shoes, but ones equipped with the most advanced technology that enhances your natural abilities. As you tighten those laces, understand that you're not just preparing for a sprint but for a marathon—a marathon through a landscape constantly reshaped by innovation and understanding.

But you're not running this marathon alone. We are in this together—running side by side—as we embrace the future. Let's be the seeds that not only grow but also flourish in this newly tilled ground. Let's be the athletes that not only run but also soar on the wings of artificial intelligence.

It's time to lace up your shoes, harness the power of technology, and embark on this journey. Let's do this, not as isolated individuals but as a united humanity, striving for a future that mirrors our highest values and aspirations.

Together, we run toward a horizon filled with the promise of what AI could be—a tool for enhancing human capability, solving complex problems, and creating a world of abundance and fairness for all.

Let's do this. Together.

Appendix: Resources for Your AI Journey

In this ever-evolving landscape of artificial intelligence, the journey to becoming proficient or even just understanding the basics can be both rewarding and overwhelming. To help you take those important first steps, here is a curated list of resources that span a range of interests and proficiency levels. Each resource mentioned can provide a solid foundation or enhance your existing knowledge base.

Personal Growth Coaching

- Pinnacle Sales Coaching: If you're looking for personalized coaching that can help you grow personally and professionally, consider checking out Pinnacle Sales Coaching. This is a resource that I personally used to level up my career and entrepreneurial journey. The insights you gain here can also be applicable as you navigate the AI landscape.
    - Website: Pinnacle Sales Coaching

Blogs and Personal Experiences

- My Alternate Dementia: In addition to the technological side of life, it's important to understand the human aspects as well. My blog provides personal insights and reflections that can enrich your journey.
    - Website: My Alternate Dementia

Professional Services

- Goalz Marketing Technologies: My company specializes in leveraging advanced technologies, including AI, for market research, branding, and more. The website contains articles, case studies, and insights into how AI is reshaping the business world. The YouTube channel is a place where you can subscribe to learn more on a bevvy of topics and ask me questions directly through the comments.
    - Website: Goalz Marketing Technologies
    - YouTube: Goalz-MKT

Online Courses and MOOCs

- Coursera: Offers a variety of courses on AI, from beginner to advanced.
- Udacity: Known for its "Nanodegree" in Artificial Intelligence.
- edX: Provides a range of courses from universities and institutions around the world.

Books

- "Artificial Intelligence: A Guide to Intelligent Systems" by Michael Negnevitsky
- "AI: A Very Short Introduction" by Margaret A. Boden
- "Life 3.0: Being Human in the Age of Artificial Intelligence" by Max Tegmark

Academic Journals

- Journal of Artificial Intelligence Research
- IEEE Transactions on Neural Networks and Learning Systems
- Artificial Intelligence Review

Online Communities

- Reddit's /r/MachineLearning
- AI Stack Exchange
- Data Science Stack Exchange

Podcasts

- Artificial Intelligence in Industry with Daniel Faggella
- The AI Podcast by NVIDIA
- Lex Fridman Podcast

Remember, the field of artificial intelligence is still young and continually evolving. No one is a master of all aspects of this technology, but with concerted effort and a willingness to keep learning, you can become a valuable player in this exciting domain.

Acknowledgments

A thank you to those who have contributed to the book and to the reader for taking this journey. A special thanks to the man who pushed my limits and challenged me to find and continue to rewrite the best version of myself, my coach and best friend.

To Byron and Rory, who left me alone to work with AI to craft this content and introduce a new generation to their generation. Our lives will be better now because of it.

Through the lens of personal experience, stark reality, and undeniable hope, this book aims to bridge the gap between fear and the incredible potential AI holds for our future. If we hold onto our essence while embracing the new, we can break free from the limitations of our fears and truly soar.

www.ingramcontent.com/pod-product-compliance
Lightning Source LLC
LaVergne TN
LVHW051743050326
832903LV00029B/2682